Self-Sabotage

*Decisions and Behaviors
That Corrode Our Lives*

Greg Moore

Prairie Papers LLC • Pueblo, Colorado

Self-Sabotage

Prairie Papers LLC
PO Box 9257
Pueblo, Colorado 81008

ISBN 978-1-7343751-2-1 (Paperback)
ISBN 978-1-7343751-3-8 (eBook)

*We have met the enemy and
he is us.*

Walt Kelly

Contents

How We Treat Others 49

Work Lives 73

Finances 89

Health and Nutrition 109

Some Final Thoughts on Finding a Better Path 131

About the Author 133

Photo Credits 135

End Notes 141

Self-Sabotage

Introduction

Fairy tales often end with the phrase: *and they lived happily ever after.* In real life, however, Little Red Riding Hood doesn't always escape the wolf, Snow White never wakes up, and Cinderella mops floors for the remainder of her life. Real life is definitely not a fairy tale, and many of us eventually reach a point where we ask ourselves in desperation: *where did things go wrong?*

Fifty years ago, the cartoonist Walt Kelly gave us a hint when he wrote "We have met the enemy and he is us."[1] His observation is helpful when thinking about how our own lives progress. We often blame our ills on others and circumstances, but realistically, we are the cause much of our own despair. We sabotage ourselves through how we think and reason, how we treat ourselves, how we treat others, how we work, how we deal with money, and how we view our health and nutrition.

Unfortunately, many of us are oblivious to the day-to-day behaviors and decisions that can cripple our lives. These are the actions and thoughts that limit opportunity, isolate us socially, keep us in perpetual

3

debt, diminish our physical well-being, and otherwise trap us in undesirable circumstances.

The corrosive behaviors and decisions discussed in this book are easy traps to fall into. Their effects can be insidious. They are often more like acid slowly eating away at pieces of metal than bullets shattering glass. Consequences build over time, often not revealing themselves for years or perhaps decades.

How can we stop self-sabotage once we recognize and take responsibility for it? One of the keys is not giving up. Not saying, "Oh well, that is just how it is going to be." Not saying, "It is too late to change." Not saying, "I don't care anymore." But instead, "I deserve better and can do better." Even small improvements should be reason for celebration. And if we have a setback one day, we can always try again tomorrow.[2]

A second factor is changing the environment. Surroundings can have an overwhelming influence on whether or not an individual can escape a self-defeating behavior. For example, a rehabilitated criminal who returns to the same environment that first led to imprisonment will likely wind up in the same bad situation again. Simply put, if we can avoid the circumstances that created the problem in the first place, our odds of success are better.

The third component is support – finding others who can provide encouragement. In some cases, this might mean professional help and guidance, while others might only require a good friend to listen and provide some objectivity. In any event, we should all steer clear of those who tell us that we can't do better.

The specific acts of self-sabotage discussed in this book are included because I have been a victim of them myself or watched helplessly as friends struggled with them. They have a decidedly American focus. My hope is that in reading this book you will find some insights that hit close to home and inspire you to make a better life for yourself and your family.

How We Think and Reason

Think Negatively

*Watch your thoughts, they become
your words;
Watch your words, they become
your actions;
Watch your actions, they become
your habits;
Watch your habits, they become
your character;
Watch your character, it becomes
your destiny.*

Lao Tzu [3]

Some of us insist on living our lives in a cloud of negativity. You probably know the type. They are always first to announce the latest bad news. They are cynical. They use "yeah, but" a lot. They are often critical of others. And they are chronic complainers. For them, the negative almost always trumps the positive. Listening to them can be a bit like getting teeth drilled.

Part of the challenge is that humans have a natural bias toward negativity. We tend to focus more on the bad than on the good. For example:

- Our memories are somewhat better for recalling bad information and events than they are for good ones.
- We react more negatively to criticism than we do positively to praise.
- We form negative stereotypes faster than we do positive ones, and those negative stereotypes are harder to change.
- We pay more attention to bad news than good news.
- We feel our losses more strongly than comparable gains cheer us.[4]

While we don't know why this bias exists, it is likely rooted in our evolution. Our ancestors were probably those who paid careful attention to potential threats.

Today, most of us could benefit from being more positive about life. But becoming more positive does not mean becoming Pollyannas who completely ignore the downside. Being concerned about issues can often compel us to do something positive about them. Similarly, considering the negative consequences of future actions is a critical part of making good decisions and forming contingency plans. But if we find ourselves constantly whining, always dismissing new ideas, repeatedly revisiting bad things from the past that we can do nothing about, or being paralyzed by fear, then it might be time to change.

Excessive negativity destroys opportunity and steers us toward unproductive paths. We are our thoughts, and as Lao Tzu explains, these can ultimately become our destiny.

Believe That We Are Smarter Than Everyone Else

Those people who think they know everything are a great annoyance to those of us who do.

Isaac Asimov [5]

We all likely know some individuals who think they are God's gift to the world. They are the ones who are fond of saying things that pad their egos. "You are lucky to have me!" "You don't know what you are talking about!" "This place would fall apart if I wasn't here!" "Don't ask questions, just do what I say!"

If we start to believe in ourselves in this way, we might want to take a few steps back because our own beliefs might not be the best basis for such an assessment. In 2000, for example, researchers at the University of Michigan showed that humans have difficultly recognizing our own incompetence, and this can lead to inflated estimates of our talent. The less competent we are in a subject, the more likely we are to overestimate our ability.[6]

We should all worry less about how smart we are and more about how much our egos are keeping us from acting on the best information, insights, and advice that we can get. The ability to reach good decisions matters far more than any IQ test result.

Make Excuses

He that is good for making excuses is seldom good for anything else.
Attributed to Ben Franklin [7]

Many of us today can't seem to take responsibility for our mistakes and failures. We always have someone else or some circumstance to blame. "The other driver stopped too quickly," instead of "I was following too closely." "I didn't complete the job on time because of the weather," instead of "I neglected to factor weather into the schedule." "I didn't pass because my teacher hates me," instead of "I didn't pass because I didn't study hard enough."

Blame shifting is counterproductive because it defers any action on our part to accept responsibility and remedy the situation. All of our energy goes into defending ourselves rather than honestly assessing our own role in the problem and doing something about it.

It is hard to be completely objective about our own shortcomings. When something bad happens to us, we tend to blame the circumstances. But when something bad happens to someone else, we tend to blame the individual.

Let Fear Dominate Our Decisions

He has not learned the lesson of life who does not every day surmount a fear.
Ralph Waldo Emerson [8]

Sometimes we refuse to do something because we are afraid of failure. Perhaps we don't ask a question in class for fear of appearing stupid. Or we don't participate in a sport because we might not be very good at it. Or we don't ask someone out to dinner because we are afraid that they will refuse our offer.

No one likes to fail, of course, but when those fears keep us from doing what we need to do to succeed or enjoy life, they become tools of self-sabotage. As the old saying goes, fear kills more dreams than failure ever has.

Failure isn't the only basis for fear. Sometimes, we worry that something terrible will happen to us physically. We don't enjoy swimming in the ocean, for example, because we saw the movie, *Jaws,* and know that a man-eating shark could show up at any time. Or we refuse to travel abroad because we believe that terrorists will get us. And while there is some chance that we will be maimed by a shark or be killed by a terrorist, neither is very likely.

Perhaps the most insidious aspect of fear is the illusion that we have no control over our fate. But we do have some control. If galeophobia (excessive fear of sharks) is keeping us from enjoying the Florida beaches, for example, we can choose to avoid shark hot spots and not swim at twilight. Similarly, we might still take that trip abroad, but avoid countries that are on the State Department's warning list.

Most of what we fear in life is learned behavior rather than something we are born with. These are the fears and anxieties that are acquired socially (parents tell their children not talk to strangers) or learned from experience (a close call during a flight). We all fear to some degree, and need some degree of fear to stay safe. But not taking that once-in-a-lifetime balloon ride because it might crash, or never running a race because we might come in last simply diminishes a life.

Accept That We Are No Good With Numbers

Math anxiety: an intense lifelong fear of two trains approaching each other at speeds of 60 and 80 mph.

Rick Bayan [9]

Consider the following problem. A train leaves Washington, DC at 7 am Eastern Daylight Time travelling west at 70 mph, and another train leaves Chicago at 8 am Central Daylight Time travelling east at 60 mph. Where will they meet on this 764 mile trip? For many would-be math students, this problem is their Waterloo. They just accept that they weren't built for numbers. And they aren't alone. Failure to compute, or "innumeracy," is pervasive in the U.S. In a recent test, for example, American students placed 30th out of 79 countries in math proficiency.[10] This is really unfortunate. Not because most Americans can't calculate the square root of 2, but because math is as much about learning to think as it is about dealing with numbers.

Math isn't easy, and we don't become proficient with numbers just by reading a book or listening to a lecture. We learn math by doing math problems and then applying the new thinking skills that we develop to decisions we make every day. The point of the two-train problem isn't really knowing where two trains meet one another somewhere in Ohio, but rather the ability to simplify a complex problem by breaking it into parts, visualizing the simpler problems and their relationship to one another, doing a calculation well within the reach of an 8th grader, and using a map to find the location.[11]

When we accept that we are no good at numbers and disregard math, we throw away a substantial and powerful part of our decision-making tools. That is good news for the credit card company that shamelessly charges 20% interest, or the politician who uses statistics to bamboozle voters. But it is bad news for us when we unwisely accept what we are being told without doing the analysis and asking the right questions.

Pay No Attention to History

A republic, if you can keep it.
Attributed to Ben Franklin [12]

As a nation, Americans are somewhat ignorant of our country's past, and particularly the sacrifices of those who preceded us. As a result, we often make decisions, support causes, and take actions that have little basis in fact. In some ways we are like Miguel de Cervantes character, Don Quixote, battling windmills because he thinks they are giants.

The difficulty with learning U.S. history is: *whose account do we choose to believe?* The words that history writers choose, how they interpret events, the stories they highlight, and the topics that they suppress all make a difference in the impression that is created about the country. Many battles have been fought by state boards of education, for example, over which version of U.S. history will be taught in the state schools.[13]

We are fortunate to live at a time when information about America's past is easily available. But as always, we should be very careful which sources we choose to believe. Many individuals and organizations have strong political, emotional, and financial reasons for wanting us to believe erroneous and misleading information.

Finding accurate and reliable information about history is hard work, but one effective strategy is to use the acronym **SIFT**.[14] **SIFT** is short for: **S**top, **I**nvestigate the source, **F**ind better coverage, and **T**race claims, quotes and media to the original context. By following this process and thinking critically, we increase the likelihood that we are not going to be influenced by poorly researched or highly-biased information.

We might become upset when we see or hear factual information about U.S. history that counters our own beliefs and values. It takes courage to accept the seamier elements of our country's past, and temper our views and beliefs because of them. While we might feel more comfortable with fabrications and misinterpretations, such beliefs are a poor basis for good citizenship and a responsible life.

Sacrifice the Future for the Now

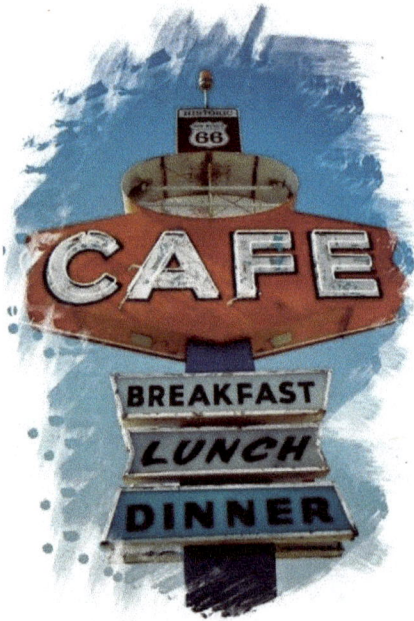

Do you go for the cheese fries or the salad?

Consistently choosing the short term over the long term is a poor life strategy. Most of us learn this important lesson when we are taught Aesop's fable of the grasshopper and the ants. The grasshopper does not worry about the future, and lives only in the moment throughout the summer. The ants, on the other hand, are busy gathering food for the coming winter. When the cold weather arrives, the grasshopper starves.

Yet many of us go through life like grasshoppers. We opt for immediate gratification, whether to gain short-term advantage or to avoid short-term struggle or inconvenience. We routinely order the French fries smothered in melted cheese rather than choosing a healthier option. We don't take the time to put on suntan lotion at the pool because we want to get into the water as soon as we can. We skip brushing our teeth at night because it is too much effort. Or we charge items that we can't afford, rather than saving now and buying later when we have the cash. Such decisions may seem largely inconsequential at the time, but when constantly repeated (as in the grasshopper's lifestyle), they can have significant consequences over the long term.

One of the more distinctive qualities of humans is that we can plan and anticipate future events. We know that eating poorly leads to health problems. We know that over-exposure to the sun leads to skin cancer. We know that our teeth will decay and fall out if we don't take care of them. And we know that spending money we don't have can ruin us financially.

We can perhaps understand and forgive the child who always opts for immediate gratification. But an adult making financial, health, and nutritional decisions should not behave as a 5-year old. The choices do matter, and short-term rewards often lead to long-term pain.

Choose Facts That Fit Our Biases

Do you see two patterns or one?

Choosing to believe only those facts that fit our biases is sometimes known as "cherry picking." The idea is that we select those cherries (or facts) that taste best (they fit our prior beliefs) and ignore the others. Any subject in which we have an emotional stake is particularly susceptible to cherry picking. Some examples are politics, race, religion, finance, and medicine.

When we no longer remain open to all sides of an issue, we begin to believe that we see the world accurately, and view anyone who disagrees with us as uninformed or naive. We see the butterfly or the two heads, but not both. Such biased thinking is a powerful form of self-sabotage because of the very narrow and limited points of view it engenders. The victims cannot correct their misbeliefs and live their lives in ignorance.

Social media has made the problem of choosing facts to fit biases far worse because it encourages like-minded individuals to form and maintain communities that simply reinforce whatever they want to believe. These groups become cocoons largely isolated from reality. Their members nurture a chosen lie, and are easy manipulated by special interest groups.

It is easy to fall into this cognitive trap. The best defense is to learn more about how humans delude themselves and try to recognize and resist those tendencies. Take a course in logic and reasoning. Join a skeptics organization or debate society. Read some highly-rated books on how humans think, such as Daniel Kahneman's *Thinking Fast and Slow* and Dan Ariely's *Predictably Irrational: The Hidden Forces That Shape Our Decisions*.[15] We can use the ideas that come from these efforts to refine our research skills, to improve our objectivity, and to learn how to better argue all sides of an issue.

Don't Learn From Mistakes

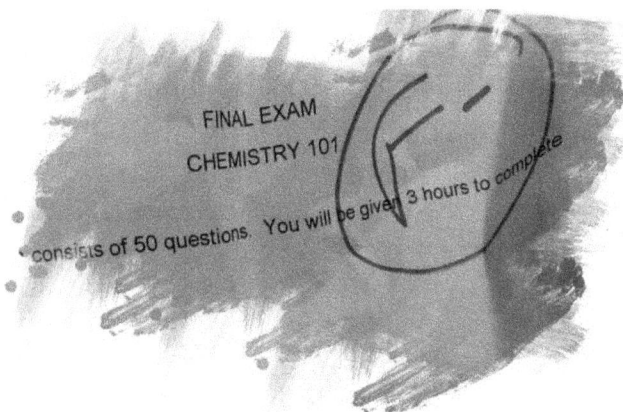

FINAL EXAM
CHEMISTRY 101
consists of 50 questions. You will be given 3 hours to complete

*Life is a series of mistakes connected by
failures to learn from them.*
Attributed to Thomas Paul [16]

Mistakes and failures are necessary facts of life. It's how we recover from them that makes all the difference.

Consider, for example, someone who gets a failing grade on a really important exam. Perhaps it is their college entrance exam, or their journeyman certification. They thought that they prepared well enough, but the test says "no way." Do they fall apart? Do they shrug it off and think: "Oh, well, there is always a job at the brick factory. Let's go get a beer?" Or do they say: "There is another test in a few months. I'll do better if I spend more time preparing. Perhaps a test preparation course or a tutor might improve my odds?"

In the first two cases, the individual learns nothing useful from the failure. They assume that they can't fix things or change things for the better. They simply accept their fate. These are acts of self-sabotage. In the third approach, on the other hand, they learn from the failure, get past the mistake, and move forward.

How We Treat Ourselves

Lie to Ourselves

My kid would never use drugs.

Sometimes in life there are warning signs about ourselves and others. Unfortunately, we often refuse to believe them because we don't like their implications.

Our once perfect child is now surly and depressed, but we are sure it is just a phase. Our aging parent, who is on several medications, seems to be out of it most of the time, but we chalk it up to normal aging. The pain we have in our abdomen isn't going away, but we are sure it's just indigestion.

Often, we deal with such problems by believing that something must be true or false not based on evidence, but on whether its consequences are acceptable to us. We reject the possibility that our child might be using drugs, for example, because it contradicts our strongly-held belief that our child is always good.

Serious problems rarely get better by denying they exist or finding a justification to avoid dealing with them effectively. An old saying goes, ignoring the signs is a good way to end up at the wrong destination.

Waste Our Education

Learning should not be a box-checking exercise.

Many of us choose to squander the public education that this country provides. Those who get the least out of the effort often do so because their only real goal is the degree. To them, the educational process is simply a box-checking exercise. Just show up and pass the tests. Unfortunately, a diploma isn't an education.

According to the U. S. Census Bureau, federal, state, and local governments spend on average over

$10,000 per student per year on public school education.[17] Governments do so because the public understands that everyone needs a basic set of facts and skills in order to survive well as adults.

Going to school can be frustrating. It is not always easy, for example, to appreciate how trigonometry or geography or Shakespeare is really preparing us for later life. But not knowing what a 45-degree angle is, or where Australia is located, or where "to be or not to be" comes from makes us (at a minimum) a bit empty-headed. We can't spend all of our time looking things up on Google.

Effective education exposes us to a wide range of subjects that are designed to be challenging. Through these experiences, we gradually develop a range of skills that include: how to read and write, how to listen, how to reason, how to ask questions, and (most importantly) how to learn on our own.[18] Without them, we are likely in for a pretty rough ride through life.

It might help to better appreciate basic education by thinking of it as a type of job, different only in that we get paid far in the future. Those future paychecks can take the form of good salaries and benefits, the people we meet, the relationships we form, and the ability to make good decisions.

Hang Out With the Wrong Crowd

It's hard to soar with the eagles when
you're surrounded by turkeys.
Longfellow Deeds [19]

We may believe that we are our own person, who thinks our own thoughts and makes our own decisions, but that is not quite true. Humans are social animals, and those with whom we associate have a substantial influence on what we believe, what we do, and ultimately, what we become.[20] If we associate with those whose view of reality is distorted, ours will become distorted too.

At some point in life, friends often become more important than family for socializing, and this gives them an outsized influence on our own behavior. If we care about our future and that of our families, we will benefit from choosing friends who can help us to become better. Those who are honest, fair, empathetic, and responsible, for example, will help us to become so as well. On the other hand, those who are self-serving, hard-hearted, mean-spirited, dishonest, self-defeating, or destructive will encourage these baser tendencies, with consequences to our health, job, relationships, and perhaps even our freedom.

Squander Our Time

He's probably not watching an educational webinar.

The father of American psychology, William James, once wrote that "My experience is what I agree to attend to. Only those items which I notice shape my mind."[21] Like James, how we spend our time will determine to a very large extent who we are and what we know. A more modern version of his idea might be *garbage in, garbage out.*[22]

How should we choose what to focus on and what to ignore? Much of this decision can be answered with the simple question: *where is this likely to lead?* Is it toward something that enriches our life, makes us or those we love happy, or improves our ability to think and reason well? Or is it something that just kills time or leads to circumstances that we will ultimately regret? If we have a choice of spending our evenings watching tv reruns or doing something productive, it should be obvious which one is self-sabotage.

This does not mean that we must fill every waking moment with a productive chore. Everyone needs time to replenish and time to explore and wander. But over the long term, we shouldn't waste our lives with insignificance. Instead, look for things that give meaning to life and to the lives of friends, family, and community.

For example, how did we spend our time during the isolation of the COVID-19 pandemic? Did we watch a lot of TV, surf the web, and play video games? Did we spend way too much time listening to half-baked breaking-news reports? Or did we think: perhaps we could use some of this time to accomplish something meaningful? Maybe it is time to dig out that guitar and learn a few songs? Or spend more time with the kids? Or learn how to cook healthier foods? Or tackle that 600-page biography of Leonardo da Vinci that we bought 3 years ago and never got around to reading? Or write a book about self-sabotage?

Steve Jobs once said that the most precious thing that we all have is time. Of course, he was a bit different than the rest of us, busy as he was creating the future with Apple computers and iPhones. But the thought is still true for all of us mere mortals.

Constantly Beat
Ourselves Up

There's a difference between telling yourself that you're not good enough and reminding yourself that there's room for improvement.

Amy Moran [23]

Psychologists can find any number of reasons why people are overly critical of themselves. But a common one is how we were raised as children. A constant flow of criticism from parents, teachers, and acquaintances can create insecurity, making us question our inherent value.[24]

When we put ourselves down or repeatedly beat ourselves up, we can dig a very deep hole. We begin to live a self-fulfilling prophesy that is full of negative thoughts, and unconsciously set ourselves up for future failures. Before long, we can't see past the edge of the hole we have dug.

When we make mistakes or fail at something that really matters, it does not mean that we are fundamentally flawed. It is only evidence that there is room for improvement. Perhaps we need to be better prepared next time, or think more deeply before we decide to act. Beyond that, beating ourselves up for every misstep we make only sabotages our chances to do better.

Let Someone Else's Addiction Ruin Our Life

Substance abuse and addiction threaten not only the addict, but those around them.

Approximately 21 million Americans are addicted either to alcohol or drugs, and a similar number of are addicted to gambling.[25] [26] Beating an addiction can be a long and arduous process. And after recovery, staying free of the addiction can be a daily battle.

Untreated addictions can not only ruin the lives of those who are afflicted, but they also adversely impact their friends and family. Physical abuse, emotional scars, untimely deaths, and financial ruin can all result from addiction. Children of parents who are addicted to alcohol or drugs are particularly vulnerable. They tend to have higher rates of mental and behavioral disorders and are more likely to become addicts themselves.[27]

The hard question is whether to stick by the addict or walk away. No one can answer that question for anyone else. But it should be clear that if our own health or that of our children is threatened, or we are codependent and want to quit, we should distance ourselves from the circumstances. Better one casualty than two or more.[28]

Defer Our Dreams Until "Someday"

30 years from now?

The problem with putting off a dream until "someday" is that "someday" has a nasty habit of never arriving. We all have responsibilities to others that we take seriously, and as a result, often put our own aspirations on hold. And while a good dose of selflessness is a virtue, absolute selflessness is not. Always putting everyone else's needs above our own is a form of self-sabotage.

Sometimes, our own dreams need to be front and center in our lives, and one way to provide this type of focus is to create a bucket list. This list contains the accomplishments and experiences that a person would like to have during their lifetime. It might include, for example, graduating from high school or college, learning a foreign language, visiting the Holy Land, running a marathon, seeing the northern lights from the Arctic Circle, reading the *Great Books of the Western World*, or becoming an accomplished ballroom dancer. Bucket lists are very personal tools that define us through our hopes and dreams.

Creating a bucket list is only the first step, however. Left on their own, those dreams remain nothing more than words on a piece of paper. If we ignore them until retirement, we will find that many of the items are physically or financially out of reach, or that we have lost the spark of enthusiasm.

A bucket list should always be a work in progress, something that is created early in life and worked on as the years progress. It is not a to-do list for retirement, but rather goals for now as well as the future. Work off some items and add new ones as time and passion permit.

Old age shouldn't be a time of would-of-could-of-should-of regret, but rather "what a ride!"

How We Treat Others

Fail to Control Our Emotions

Silence speaks so much louder than screaming.

Taylor Swift [29]

How well we understand our emotions, how we use them, and how we control them is known as emotional intelligence. Six-year-olds can be forgiven for having poor emotional intelligence because they are just learning. But some adults never learn to control childhood emotions. They never fully grasp

51

that the world does not revolve around them, and continue to treat others as if it does.

Here are some examples that we have all likely observed on occasion:

- Giving another driver the finger because they are going too slowly.
- Yelling at someone when things don't happen to go our way.
- Firing off an offensive email or Tweet in response to something we disagree with.
- Denigrating someone behind their back.
- Damaging someone's property to get back at them.
- Threatening to physically harm someone.
- Being disrespectful of a speaker with whom we disagree.

Such behaviors are almost always damaging to potential and existing relationships. Later apologies rarely erase the damage completely.

There is a bit of the 6-year-old in each of us. When it starts to emerge, we need to take Archie Bunker's advice and "stifle it."[30]

Meddle in Other's Lives

Do not meddle in the affairs of dragons,
for you are crunchy and good with
ketchup. [31]

"Meddle" is a great word. It means that we can't resist sticking our nose where it doesn't belong. The parent who can't resist criticizing their grown children's parenting skills. The neighborhood busybody who calls out anyone for the slightest issue. The eavesdropper who can't resist offering advice. The overzealous political groupie who just can't stop telling others how they should vote. While all of these meddlers may believe they have our best interests at heart, rarely does the result justify the intrusion on what is clearly someone else's business.

When we meddle, we annoy others and undermine our own prospects. Meddling in family issues is a frequent source of familial tensions. Meddling in social situations prevents casual acquaintances from ever developing further into friendships. Meddling at work destroys worker confidence and causes resentment and frustration. Meddling with complete strangers can get someone shot.

Instead of intruding on others' business, we should focus on what we can do to put our own lives in better order. As the philosopher, Eric Hoffer, noted: "A man is likely to mind his own business when it is worth minding. When it is not, he takes his mind off his own meaningless affairs by minding other people's business."[32]

Ignore the Rules

An opportunistic target on a rural road in Colorado.

If someone asks us if we are excellent drivers, what would we say? Most of us would probably say "yes," but many of us would be wrong. Rule-breaking behaviors like texting while driving, speeding, tailgating, weaving in and out of traffic, rubber necking, driving while feeling drowsy, and running stop signs are common everyday events.

Mostly, drivers get away with such misbehavior. But sometimes there are consequences. In the U.S., over 6 million automobile accidents typically occur every year. As a result, approximately 37,000 adults and children die and 3 million more are injured. For the most part, these deaths and injuries are caused by drivers who simply chose to ignore basic rules of the road.[33]

Driving safely and civilly is just one of many established norms in society that exist to keep things running efficiently and protect us. We might not like such rules, but they are the price we pay so that 330 million people can (for the most part) live together without killing each other. When we openly break rules, we effectively advertise to the world that we aren't to be trusted. Not a reputation that any thoughtful person should seek.

The caution sign that is peppered with bullet holes is a simple example. The sign exists to alert drivers of a safety concern, not to provide recreation for some frustrated shooter. Most people who use firearms understand that one of the basic rules is to avoid shooting when the background is uncertain. Whoever decided to use the sign as a target apparently didn't care much at the time about safe use of firearms or the lives he or she potentially endangered on that country road.

Not all rules are good or fair, of course, and these should be questioned, protested, and changed. The key is making sure that we fully understand what we are doing. Why does the rule exist? How are people harmed and how do people benefit from its elimination? A good test of how well we understand a rule is to see if we can coherently argue both for and against it.

We all have a growing responsibility to work toward meaningful change in a world that is increasingly crowded and threatened. But ignoring societal rules just because we don't like them or just "feel like it" is largely a statement of selfishness, narrow-mindedness, and ignorance.

Obsess Over Rights and Ignore Responsibilities

The right to swing a fist ends where the other person's nose begins.

As Americans, we often seem to be far more concerned about someone trampling on our rights than accepting the duties and responsibilities that go along with those rights. This lopsided obsession is, at the very least, selfish, and often self-defeating. Lives are diminished and sometimes ruined when rights are irresponsibly exercised.

For example, it is the right of adult Americans to have children if they so choose. Currently, there are approximately 78 M children aged 0 to 17 in the U.S. and approximately 3.8 M more are born each year.[34] [35] The majority of American adults have children at some time during their lives.

But along with this right comes the responsibility to care well for those children physically, emotionally, and educationally. Unfortunately, too many today seem to think that this responsibility is optional. In the U.S., for example:

- By some estimates, more than 11 M children live in homes with insufficient food.[36]
- Approximately 700,000 children were victims of child abuse in 2018. Of these victims, 1770 of them died from the abuse.[37]
- In families where parents divorce, almost half of parents owed child support do not receive full payments.[38]
- Repeated surveys show that parents are largely clueless about their children's education.[39]
- Childhood diseases due to unhealthy eating habits are on the rise.[40]

Many nations of the world rate far better than the U.S. in raising children, despite the advantages that this country offers.

When we fail to meet our duties to our children, or shirk other responsibilities like voting, being faithful to our marriage vows, following health guidelines during a crisis, and obeying the law, others must deal with the messes that we create. Ignoring responsibility puts us solidly in that class of society's bottom feeders who constantly take without giving anything meaningful back.

As Winston Churchill once noted, "The price of greatness is responsibility."[41]

Act Like a Know-It-All

While it is often said that honesty is the best policy, silence is the second best policy.

Criss Jami [42]

Are you one of those folks who frequently says: *You don't know what you are talking about?* The statement roles off of the tongue nicely, doesn't it? Unfortunately, it is one of the more toxic comments we can make to anyone.

How we approach criticism and argument almost always matters, and it deserves some deep thought.

61

For example, inundating others with facts to support a cherished position or belief rarely changes anyone's mind. Better approaches almost always involve a deeper understanding of motives and beliefs. As Peter Boghossian and James Lindsay note in their book, *How to Have Impossible Conversations*, "...the discussion appears to be about issues, ideas, and facts, but instead it's really about the type of person the entrenched person perceives herself to be."[43]

How we approach criticism is especially important for conflicts between parents and children and bosses and employees. Parents who point out the flaws in their children without first considering the best way to motivate them, for example, aren't really helping. More likely, their criticisms are simply building a gap that will be difficult to bridge in the future. In a similar vein, bosses who bluntly correct employees often do irreparable damage to morale and trust.

As Dale Carnegie once wrote: "When we are wrong, we may admit it to ourselves. And if we are handled gently and tactfully, we may admit it to others and even take pride in our frankness and broad-mindedness. But not if someone else is trying to ram the unpalatable fact down our esophagus."[44]

Spend More Time Talking Than Listening

It is better to remain silent at the risk of being thought a fool, than to talk and remove all doubt of it.

Maurice Switzer [45]

We all probably know someone who can't stop talking. I can still recall one encounter years ago with a chatterbox who went on continuously for more than 15 minutes. When I finally made a comment to try to get the meeting back on topic, her reaction was: "don't interrupt me, I am not finished talking."

When someone is more interested in their own words than those of others, they are unlikely to learn anything new and useful. Bernard Baruch was an influential 20th century financier and economic advisor to several U.S. Presidents. He wisely observed that most of the successful people he'd known were the ones who did more listening than talking.[46]

Being a good listener means, at a minimum, respecting the speaker. Showing that we are interested and paying attention. Asking good questions. Focusing on what they are saying, not on what we would like to say next.

Swear Incessantly

Under certain circumstances, urgent circumstances, desperate circumstances, profanity provides a relief denied even to prayer.

Mark Twain [47]

Why do we swear? Often it is to express feelings and emotions and, used sparingly, it can be an effective tool. For example, studies have shown that swearing can ease pain.[48] Used in just the right way, swearing can also convey power, authenticity, an appropriate degree of rebellion, and directness.[49]   But those findings should not be an open invitation to constant gratuitous vulgarity and profanity.

Anyone can hurl a string of profanities under the right circumstances (like slamming the door on a finger). But it takes a really foul person to keep it up in every sentence they utter. We've all run into these guys and gals. Every other word they utter is profane. "F**k" is for some reason their favorite noun, adverb and adjective. While such behavior draws attention, it is not generally the kind of attention that will help someone go far in life. We can't easily establish positive relationships or learn much of value when we create a barrier that is offensive to most people.

Fail to Meet
Commitments

You get your first job on your ability and every job after that on your dependability.

Mike Royer [50]

Organizations and societies rely in great measure on those who are reliable. These are the people who take their commitments seriously. They show up on time, they prepare well, and they keep their promises.

On the other hand, those who take a casual view of their commitments often place burdens on others. If we don't show up for work on time, other employees have to pick up the slack. If we don't deliver our part of the project when we promised it, the team effort risks failure. If our work is careless and sloppy, others have to correct it. Failure to fulfill commitments leaves a trail of debris that others have to make right.

While being dependable is primarily a form of respect to others, it can also convey personal benefits. When we gain a reputation for meeting commitments, more and better opportunities will come our way. Chances are that those new opportunities will also come with more freedom of action, because people know that they don't have to keep a constant eye on us.

No one should want to be the weak link in a chain. An old saying goes, "Reliability leads to indispensability; unreliability leads to irrelevance."

Don't Control a Short Fuse

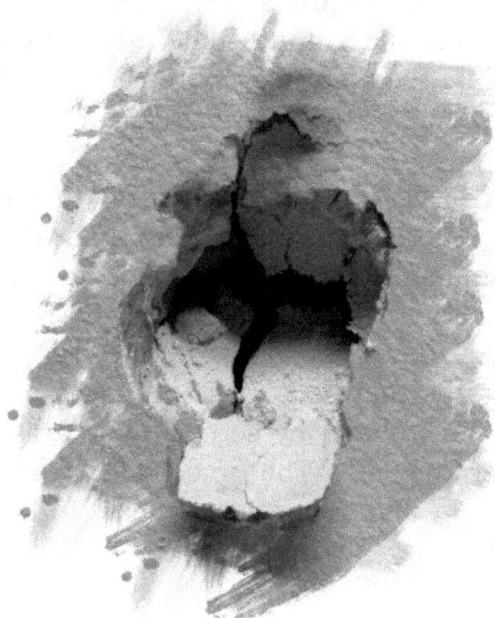

Better a piece of wallboard than someone's nose.

The comedian Groucho Marx once said "Speak when you are angry and you will make the best speech that you will ever regret."[51] When we can't control our tempers, friendships are lost, opportunities evaporate, and people get hurt.

According to the Mayo Clinic, some strategies that can help control a short fuse include: thinking before we open our mouths, taking a break to calm down, and learning relaxation skills. Using humor to release tension and getting some exercise can also help.[52] While these strategies are easy to list, they have to be practiced regularly to be of any use.

Anger is a basic survival mechanism that can be healthy or unhealthy, depending on what we do with it. When someone cuts us off in traffic, for example, threatening them with our vehicle is a recipe for disaster. On the other hand, getting angry at the morning traffic that makes us chronically late and resolving the problem by setting the alarm a half hour earlier is smart. The first strategy can get us shot or put in jail. The second helps to keep the paycheck coming.

Fail to Launch

*I wonder if Mom has done
my laundry yet?*

Failure to launch is a relatively recent phrase that refers to the difficulty some young adults have in achieving independence and responsibility. The effect is often stereotyped as the unemployed 25-year son who is entrenched in his parents' basement playing video games. For whatever reasons (such as a sense of entitlement, poor social skills, substance abuse, permissive parents, etc.), the parent-child umbilical cord remains firmly in place long past its expiration date.

71

Young adults need to cut the cord at some point in order to grow and thrive. One of the biggest benefits of college, for example, is that it finally gets children out of the house and (at least a bit) on their own. Ideally, they will have developed adequate skills for independence by graduation, and their parents can finally convert that bedroom into an office or den. Military service can serve the same purpose.

Help is available for those dealing with adult children who can't make the leap. For example, failure-to-launch programs and counseling services exist throughout the country that can provide young adults with the knowledge and confidence they need to be on their own. It is critical that parents not succumb to the ideas that their adult children "will grow out of it," or "won't love me anymore," or "still need my help."[53]

A parent's primary job is usually complete once their children have gained a basic education and living skills. They don't owe them a place to stay, money to live on, or emotional support for every decision that needs to be made. They do, however, owe their children the respect to let them live and succeed or fail on their own.

Work Lives

Never Graduate From High School

Home Sweet Home for far too many high school dropouts.

Dropping out of high school often puts a person at a disadvantage that can last a lifetime. On average, for example, dropouts earn 25-30% less than high school graduates.[54] Not graduating can also be a fast track to jail. According to the *Fight Crime: Invest in Kids* organization: "High school dropouts are three and one-half times more likely than high school graduates to be arrested, and more than eight times as likely to be incarcerated."[55] Dropping out is not a guarantee that someone will earn less or wind up in jail, but not graduating does put them on a path that makes such fates more likely.

There are always exceptions, of course. Dave Thomas (the founder of Wendy's), Peter Jennings (an ABC news anchor) and Richard Branson (founder of Virgin Airlines), all dropped out of high school. But making a decision to quit school because it worked out really well for a few who did is a bad bet. By definition, most people will not be the exception to the rule.

Students typically drop out for 3 basic reasons: (1) factors within the school environment that push them out, such as disciplinary policies; (2) factors external to the school that pull them out, such as having to support a family; or (3) a general lack of progress and increasing apathy and disillusionment with school.[56] While some will always choose to drop out, support and encouragement from parents, relatives, teachers, friends, and organizations can make a difference.[57]

Work for a Jerk

Memo to self: get a new job.

How do we know if we work for a jerk? Stanford University professor Robert Sutton has made a career studying jackasses, and his answer is simple. Do they make us feel like dirt? Do they demean us? Do they disrespect us? Do they suck the energy out of us?[58]

Almost all of us wind up working for a bad boss at some point in our lives. But we should never let it go on for too long. Many bad bosses have no problem sacrificing others for their own gain. In addition, being a jerk can be contagious. Work for one long enough, and some of those undesirable characteristics will likely rub off on us.

What can we do when our great boss is replaced with an ass? In the short term, we can try to focus on the positive aspects of the job, do what we can to minimize hot buttons, and find ways to relieve the stress. If possible, we can also try to lay low, add some physical distance, or perhaps take a temporary assignment somewhere else. If things don't improve, then we probably need to find a better boss.

It can be tough to walk away from what was once a good job, but here is a trick that might help. Write two job descriptions, one for what the job was like before the new boss took over, and one for what it is like now. Be sure to include a description of the work environment. For example, if the new boss yells frequently, include something like "serve as gratuitous punching bag" in the job description, because the job now includes providing that stress relief. Also include any prospects for advancement, since these have undoubtedly changed as well.

Now compare the two descriptions. Do the good parts still outweigh the bad? Is this new job one we would every apply for? In answering such questions, we must try to not fall prey to the *sunk cost fallacy* (thinking we have too much invested to leave) or put too much stock in *false hope* (believing that things will get better on their own).

Choose the Wrong Line of Work

What You Are
Good At
What You Can
Get Paid For
What You Like
To Do
Aim Here

A simple career formula. Choose the intersection of what we are good at, what we like to do, and what others will pay us to do.

Far too often, we simply fall into our careers or are nudged into them by others. Many of us later come to regret the decision, realizing too late that we've missed a window of opportunity and are stuck with the consequences. It is easy to spot victims of poor career decisions. They go to work, but rarely with enthusiasm, pride and satisfaction. Starting over is often possible, of course, but it is never easy.

If there is one decision that we should think deeply about and make largely on our own, it is the occupation we want to pursue. The drawing on the previous page provides a general way to think about the problem. It is a Venn diagram. Each of the circles represents a key element of a successful career.

The best chance of a career that we will like and will stay with lies where all three elements intersect: what we are good at, what we like to do, and what others will pay us to do. All three must be true. For example, we can be pretty good at something we like to do (such as playing video games), but may never get someone to pay us well to do it. On the other hand, we might really like a popular and well-paying job (playing baseball or acting, for example), but are not good enough to make a living from it. Or, we might be good at a job that pays well (a tax accountant or salesman, perhaps), but not really like the work. The diagram is ours and ours alone. Everyone has different skills and preferences.

Of course, the process is not foolproof, and this is where others can help. As humans, we are very good at overestimating what we are good at and often give far too much weight to what we might like to do or think we should be paid. In such cases, objective outside opinions from those who know us and know an occupation can often prevent a poor decision.

Similarly, internships and other hands-on experiences can go a long way toward finding clear answers to the questions in the Venn diagram.

And what if we choose poorly? Berkshire Hathaway CEO Warren Buffett has this advice: "In a chronically leaking boat, energy devoted to changing vessels is more productive than energy devoted to patching leaks."[59]

Steal From Employers

They'll never notice. And besides, they don't pay me what I am worth.

It's hard to imagine a more effective way to sabotage ourselves than by stealing from the company we work for. While it may be that no one really cares if we have taken a few office supplies from work, crimes like time-card fraud, robbing the till, using office computer systems for illicit purposes, and misuse of data are fast tracks to unemployment or worse.

There is no upside to such activities. Not only do they threaten our current job, but the consequences could haunt us for years and eliminate us from some types of jobs entirely. Theft destroys reputations that take years to build. Why would anyone trust us in the future?

Do Less Than Our Best

Talent is never enough. With few exceptions the best players are the hardest workers.

Magic Johnson [60]

When we buy something at the store, we expect to get our money's worth. The situation is no different for an employer who is paying us a reasonable salary to do a job. They expect and deserve a best effort.

But the benefits of doing our best are not just conveyed to the person who signs our paycheck.

Those who do the work are often the largest beneficiary of their effort. When we make good work the norm, we tend to get better at what we do. And good work gets noticed, often leading to bigger opportunities.

It is easy to do a job well when we believe in it, and much harder when we don't. There is a popular story about a visit to NASA by former U.S. President John Kennedy. During his visit, the President saw a janitor at work and asked him what he was doing. The janitor replied: "Well, Mr. President, I'm helping to put a man on the moon."[61]

If we can't view our current job in a meaningful way, then it might time for a change. Simply hanging on for the sake of a check is unfair to the employer and a waste of opportunity for the employee.

Let Our Job Become Our Life

*A man should never neglect
his family for business.*

Walt Disney [62]

Some of us see our job as our life. We always come to work early and leave late. We skimp on vacations and use weekends and holidays to catch up on work. When asked about ourselves, we mostly talk about our jobs rather than our family or other outside interests. Overall, we place a far lower day-to-day priority on other uses of our time.

In the end, all jobs are temporary, so putting most of one's self-worth into one makes little sense. Our lives have multiple dimensions and all of them (family, friends, community, work, charity, self-development, relaxation, etc.) deserve some of our time and effort. Losing a job should not mean losing everything that matters.

Ironically, those who put all of their waking efforts into their jobs are not necessarily more productive than those with balanced lives. There is strong evidence, for example, that well-planned vacations improve productivity and mental health.[63] Yet more than half of all working Americans don't use all of their allotted vacation days each year.[64] And when they do go on vacation, too many bring along a computer "just to check in occasionally."

We all need time to recharge. As author Stephen Covey explains, not doing so is like trying to saw lumber with a dull saw. The longer we go, the harder each stroke becomes. Eventually, more smoke and char are being produced than sawdust. On the other hand, if we take a bit of time to sharpen the saw teeth, progress is far easier.[65]

Finances

Spend Every Cent We Earn

Financial security is less about how much we make than much we save.

One of the principles of financial management is maintaining a solid emergency fund to sustain a family through a costly health issue or a job loss. Experts suggest that a reasonable number to shoot for is 3 to 6 months of essential expenses. This includes items such as monthly mortgage or rent, utilities, food, insurance, transportation, education, debt payments, etc.

A single person living in an apartment in Denver, Colorado, for example, might spend on the order of $1500 per month on rent plus $1000 on other essentials. Covering these expenses for 6 months would require an emergency fund of $15,000.[66]

Unfortunately, the majority of American adults are unprepared to deal with any significant financial emergency. A 2019 GOBankingRates survey revealed that 69% of adults have less than $1000 in savings, hardly enough to carry them for a few days, let alone months. Almost half of those who responded to the survey had no savings at all.[67]

Yet many of us dutifully line up at Starbucks each morning for a Venti Caramel Macchiato at $4.75 plus a slice of banana nut bread at $2.75. That habit, repeated for 5 days per week and 50 weeks per year will cost $1875, *after taxes*. And no, it is not a deductible business expense just because it is the only thing that gets us out of bed and to work.

That is not meant as a ding on Starbucks. Any company that can convince a consumer that $4.75 plus tip is a fair price for a cup of coffee deserves our respect. But it does illustrate how easily we can fall into the trap of daily spending for what should be at best an occasional treat.[68] Over time, we let many of the things we want morph into things we can't seem to do without.

One of the most important principles of financial freedom is that we should always pay ourselves first. A good way to do that is to develop the habit of saving the first 10 percent of every after-tax paycheck. This strategy works best when the funds are withdrawn automatically, reducing the temptation to spend them.

It might help to think of enforced savings this way. When we live on only 90% of our take-home paycheck for the 14 days in a pay period, that 10% we just put away is buying 1.56 work-free days that we can cash in during an emergency. Since there are roughly 26 pay periods in a year, the emergency fund we create in just one year will cover approximately 40 days, or a bit more than 5 ½ weeks.[69]

Nothing conveys freedom like a buck in the bank.

Maintain Balances on Credit Cards

Compound interest is the 8th wonder of the world. He who understands it, earns it; he who doesn't, pays it.
Attributed to Albert Einstein [70]

Whether Einstein really said that compound interest was the 8th wonder of the world doesn't matter nearly as much as whether we understand the power of interest and time.

Let's say that we borrow $10,000 at an interest rate of 10%. The interest is compounded yearly, and we agree to pay the $10,000 back with accumulated interest at the end of 5 years. When the loan comes due, we'd write a check for $16,105. If the interest rate had been 5% instead of 10%, the check would have been $12,763. If the 10% loan been for a longer period, perhaps 10 years instead of 5, the check would have been for $25,937.

How much we borrow, the interest rate we pay, how often the interest is compounded, and how long the loan lasts all contribute the price we pay to borrow money. These factors can sabotage any budget, especially when they involve credit card balances.

In 2020, the average credit card debt in the United States was $6,194 and the average interest rate (APR) on that debt was 21.21%.[71] Assuming that a cardholder made a minimum 3% payment each month, it would take over 21 years to pay the debt in full. During that time, the borrower would pay $14,621. The finance charges alone would be $8,427, far more that the original amount owed.[72]

But what about those wonderful points that credit card issuers offer? The free airline tickets, the double points on restaurants, and the free stuff on Amazon? While these may look like bargains, they are all sucker bait. If our decision to add to credit card debt is *ever* influenced by the points it will generate, we are in the self-sabotage business.

One of the best ways that we can improve our finances is to pay off our credit card balances every month. While this is a good goal, emergencies will likely occur in which we have to violate this rule. But starting from a zero-debt balance is always better than piling debt on already existing debt.

Put All of Our Eggs in One Basket

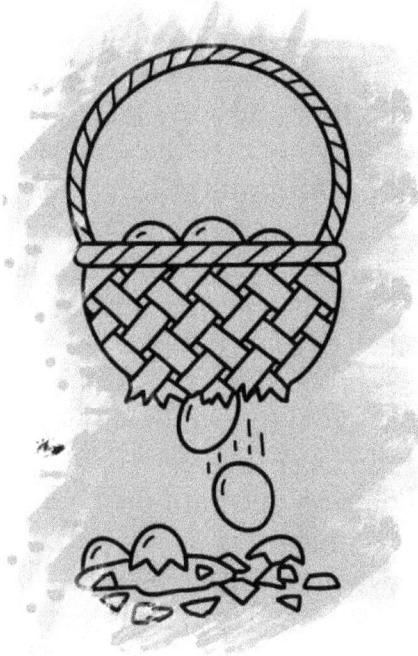

Do we have a Plan B?

We all have heard the old adage that we should not put all of our eggs in one basket, but what does that really mean? The basic idea is that putting all of our eggs in one basket is efficient and the easiest way to manage them, but if something goes wrong (the basket breaks or we drop it), we lose them all. We have no backup. No plan B. A safer strategy is to diversify — to have more baskets — in case one of them fails.

Diversification is a form of risk management most often associated with financial investments such as stock and bond portfolios. Putting all of our retirement savings in our company stock, for example, would be considered poor diversification. It is a bad strategy because the company could fail sometime in the future, and we could lose everything we've invested. A diversified investment plan, on the other hand, would include owning a variety of stocks and bonds. While one or two might fail over time, the chances of all of them failing is low.

Many things we do in life require diversification as a form of protection against catastrophe. Storing all of our personal data on one hard drive without remote backup, for example, puts us at risk of losing all of our data in a fire or theft. Using the same password for all of our accounts turns one costly hack into many. Relying on two incomes to pay the mortgage means that one job loss could cost us the house we live in. In each case, if something goes wrong, all of the eggs will lie broken on the pavement. Perhaps things will be okay and nothing bad will happen, but do we really want to count on that?

Play Roulette With Health Insurance

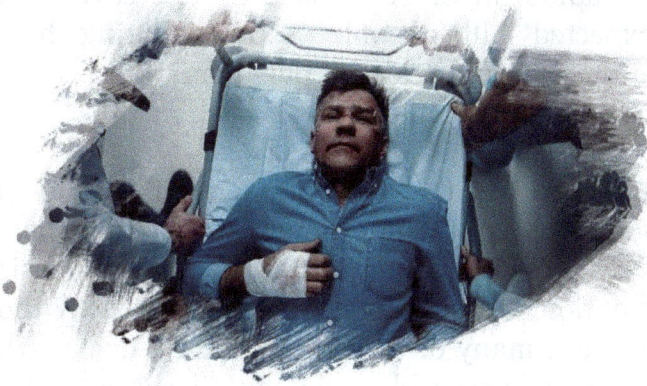

*How am I ever going
to pay for this?*

In the United States, approximately 26.1 million people had no health insurance at any time during 2019. Since there are roughly 325 million of us, that makes a bit less than 1 in 12. Texas had the highest uninsured rate (18.4 percent, or roughly 1 in 5) and Massachusetts had the lowest (3.0 percent, or roughly 1 in 33).[73]

When we skimp on health insurance, we sabotage ourselves in two ways. The first is financial. Approximately 2/3rds of all bankruptcies in 2019 were due to medical expenses.[74] Without health insurance, even a simple broken arm that doesn't require surgery could cost $2500. If surgery is needed, the bill could be $16,000 or more.[75] Since 4 in 10 adults in the U.S. have trouble covering an unexpected bill of only $400, ignoring health insurance would clearly put many of us on a destructive financial path.[76]

The second way that skipping health insurance can sabotage us is by compromising our future health and well-being. Today's health care emphasizes prevention and detecting conditions early. Without insurance, many of us will only visit a doctor if we have an obvious problem like a toothache or a broken arm. Yet the ability to deal with many medical conditions (such as gum disease, sleep disorders, diabetes, heart disease, and colon cancer) benefits greatly from early detection. The longer such conditions go unchecked, the harder it is to recover from them or survive with them.

There is no age at which it is okay to forgo health insurance. While some may think of health insurance as wasted money because they are young and healthy and believe that nothing bad is going to happen to them, that is wishful thinking. Accidents happen, and increasingly, the diseases of older adults like type 2 diabetes, stroke, high blood pressure and cancer are showing up in younger generations. We should always purchase insurance in the hope that we will never need it.

America has a bit of built-in insanity in the way we tie health insurance to jobs. While health insurance is a very nice benefit for those whose jobs provide it, this can create a double whammy for those who are fired or laid off. According to AARP, most employers pay 70-80% of the cost of health insurance and the employee plays the remainder.[77] If the employee's share of his or her annual health insurance premiums is $1200, for example, the employer might be providing $4800. Knowing this, we should always be prepared to go it alone for a time, if needed. Any reliable emergency fund plan should have health insurance as a line item.

Run Up College Debt

*A path to a successful career
or to endless debt?*

A college education is not cheap. In 2019, the average cost of tuition and fees at a public college was $10,116 per year. Private colleges averaged $36,801.[78] Even with grants and scholarships, the odds are that going to college will still involve borrowing money. Approximately two-thirds of those who graduated from college in 2018, for example, financed some portion of the experience with federal or private loans. The average amount owed on graduation was $29,200.[79]

Most colleges charge the same tuition, no matter which major is chosen. As a result, the salaries that will ultimately pay off that college debt over time can vary quite a bit, perhaps requiring 5% of annual income in one case and 25% in another.[80] Clearly, choice of major should matter a great deal in terms of how much debt is acceptable. The ten majors with the highest starting salaries are mostly engineering degrees. The lowest include early childhood education, social work, and theology.[81]

We should always "do the math" ahead of time. For example, it might not make sense to run up a great deal of debt for a degree that does not typically lead to a well-paying career. The key question is: *given a reasonable salary for this major, how many years will it take to pay off my college debt?* While the standard federal repayment plan for a student loan is 10 years, the average payoff period is roughly twice that. So, on average, if we graduate at 22 years old, chances are that we'll be in our forties before we make our last payment.[82]

College can be a ticket to a better life, but it also can be a ticket to a financial fiasco.

Have Children Too Early in Life

The maternity bill is just a down payment.

The folk singer James Taylor says that there are three things in life that will enslave us. One is addiction. One is debt. And the last is having children before we are ready to support them.[83]

Age matters in our decisions if and when to have children, both from the standpoint of maturity and finances. Those who get married in their teens, for example, are twice as likely to get divorced within 10 years as those who marry in their late twenties.[84] And when teenagers have babies, those children are far more likely to be abused, to drop out of school, and to wind up in prison.[85]

Raising children is expensive at any age. According to the U.S. Department of Agriculture, the average cost of raising one child through the age of 17 is approximately $250,000, or almost $15,000 per year.[86] Food, shelter, medical visits, insurance – it all adds up fast. Any hopes of sending a son or daughter to college are on top of that $250,000.

Don't Plan for Emergencies

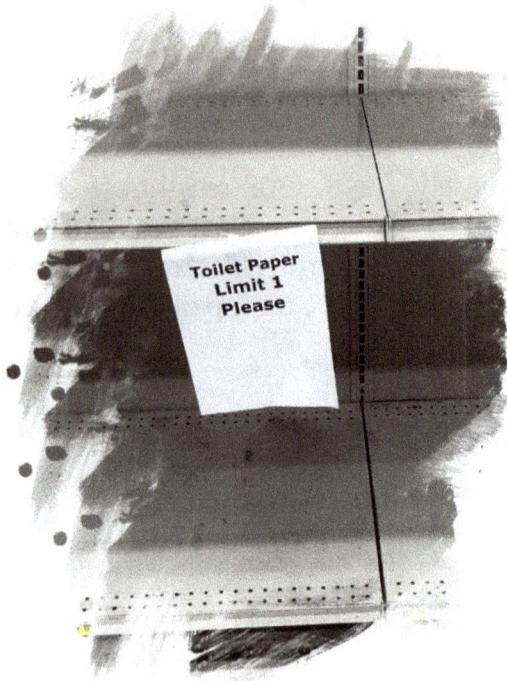

How some Americans plan for emergencies.

When a crisis occurs, some of us always seem to part of the problem rather than part of the solution. We are the ones who raid the supermarket for toilet paper at the last moment, who arrogantly decide to "ride out" the hurricane instead of evacuating, or use the ER for every sickness rather than finding a family doctor or clinic.

Humans consider themselves different from other animals in that we have highly-developed abilities to anticipate the future and plan for it. Those who want to minimize their chances of self-sabotage should use that ability as much as they can.

Here are a few things that we should all think through carefully and often:

- Future loss of a job and its effect on income needed to pay expenses.
- A potential national or local emergency that requires evacuation or sheltering in place.
- The possibility of a family member's chronic illness that requires outside help.
- Our own death (more on this later).

Former President Eisenhower, who led the largest land assault in history on D-Day during WWII, always liked to remark that a plan is useless, but planning is everything.[87] The process of thinking through a problem and considering possible outcomes means that when an actual emergency unfolds, a good planner will have created some contingencies and will be better prepared to deal with it.

Health and Nutrition

Take Up Smoking

*Smoking is just paying
a corporation to kill you.*

Our grandparents and great-grandparents can be forgiven for taking up smoking. In their time, no one really knew how dangerous it was. After all, the tobacco companies were pretty convincing with their "More Doctors Prefer Camels!" advertisements. And those movie stars did look pretty sophisticated with a cigarette dangling from their fingers.

We now have the benefit of experience and better medical knowledge. And despite all of the tobacco industry's efforts to sow doubt, we now know that smoking offers a quicker trip to the grave, not only for the smoker, but also for those who live around them. According to the CDC, approximately 16 million Americans are living with diseases caused by smoking, and about a half-million of them die each year. Second-hand smoke alone is responsible for about 41,000 deaths per year, or more than die in car accidents.[88]

Smoking is a hard addiction to beat, and one has to have some sympathy for those who want to quit but cannot shake the habit. But anyone who starts smoking today because of peer pressure or other factors is just sabotaging themselves.

Even if health is not a concern, surely the financial burden must mean something. Across the U.S. today, the average pack of cigarettes costs $6.96.[89] If regular smokers use a pack a day and are employed for the 2020 federal minimum wage of $7.25 an hour, they each work more than an hour a day for those cigarettes.

Eat Whatever We Like

Two fried glazed donuts, a burger, and bacon, plus a side of greasy fries. Can you feel your arteries hardening just looking at this picture?

In the 1996 film, *Michael*, John Travolta plays the archangel whose most noteworthy nutritional advice is that "no matter what they tell you, you can *never* have too much sugar!"[90] While that might work for an immortal, it is pretty bad nutritional advice for the rest of us.

Depending on activity level, adult women in their 40s need somewhere between 1,800 and 2,200 calories per day, while adult men in the same age group need 2,200 to 2,800 calories.[91] That donut bacon burger and fries is almost enough for an entire day.

Of course, it is not just the calories that matter. Our bodies need energy, but they also need the right materials to build and regenerate our bodies. If we avoid vitamin C, for example, we will contract scurvy. Eventually, our gums will swell, our teeth will fall out and we'll become bedridden.[92] Similarly, a lack of vitamin D and calcium can severely weaken our bones and teeth, and a lack of fiber can increase our risk of diabetes and heart disease.[93]

The internet can be a dangerous place to seek nutritional information unless we know where to look. Anyone, for example, can create a website and call themselves a nutritionist. Better information on basic food and nutrition comes from credible sources such as licensed dieticians and science-based web sites. The latter include the Mayo Clinic and the USDA's Food and Nutrition Information Center.[94] While these sources don't know everything, they contain more trustworthy advice than those that are simply trying to make a buck selling the latest gimmick with a splashy headline or irresistible clickbait.[95]

The earlier in life that we decide to start eating well, the better our long-term health is likely to be. And if we need motivation, we simply need to look around.

Handle Stress Poorly

I...must...have...pie.

We all deal with stress in different ways, and some are better at it than others. But if our personal strategy involves booze, junk food, a joint, binge shopping, or taking it out on others, we are clearly not handling pressure all that well.

The primary sources of stress for most of us today are more likely to be mental rather than physical. Marriage, divorce, death, loss of a job, family health problems, issues at work, and debt are some of the external challenges that we meet in life. Other sources of stress are within us — our fears and anxieties and expectations.

There are many different ways to cope with stress. The Mayo Clinic, for example, suggests thinking in terms of the 4 A's:

- *Avoid* stresses. We should learn to say no when we are too busy to take on new responsibilities. We should minimize contact with circumstances that stress us out.
- *Alter* the situation. We should speak up when we are frustrated. We should manage our time better.
- *Accept* things that we can't change. We should learn to forgive and place things in larger perspective.
- *Adapt*. We should adjust our expectations. In the end, does something really matter?

These techniques require some practice. They are not cure-alls, but once learned, they can create a stronger foundation for handling whatever life throws at us.[96] A trusted friend who listens well can also help.

There is no such thing as a stress-free life. Rather than hope for one, we should work toward a life in which we manage stress well. We should expect problems to occur and deal with them constructively. If we handle one stressful situation well, we are more likely to see the next one as simply another challenge that we can calmly deal with.

Become a Couch Potato

You'd think a class act like me would have better things to do.

Here's a test. We've just had a big meal, and that couch in front of the television looks really good. It is beckoning us, and we have a tough decision to make: do we sit and watch TV, or do we take a walk? Studies show that we are more likely to choose the couch option.[97]

A sedentary life is a sabotaged life for many reasons. Health problems such as heart disease, stroke, diabetes, osteoporosis and some types of cancer are all linked to inactivity. A lack of physical activity also amplifies mental health issues such as depression and anxiety. Finally, being inactive can limit our enjoyment of life's experiences and opportunities. Instead of experiencing life as an active explorer, we tend to become mere spectators. We watch golf instead of playing it. We experience a national park from the turnouts on the road, rather than hiking its trails. We don't take the bus tour because it is too difficult to get in and out of the vehicle. We are too creaky to have the joy of tending a garden.

A sedentary life is a tough habit to break. But it is a habit, and habits can be changed. Start small — perhaps by parking at the far end of the grocery store parking lot rather than battling others for spots near the door. Take the stairs at work rather than riding the elevator. Buy an exercise bike and peddle through a favorite tv program.

The old Chinese proverb that a journey of 1000 miles begins with a single step can be good advice for beating a couch potato lifestyle.

Disregard Our Doctor's Advice

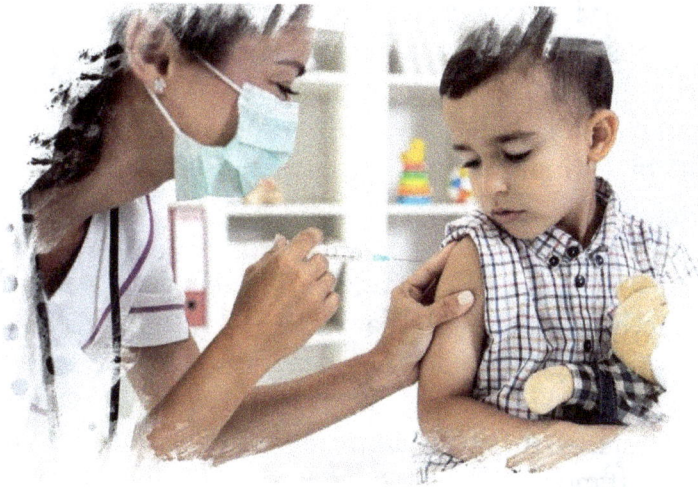

In 1966, 73 percent of Americans said they had great confidence in the leaders of the medical profession. In 2012, only 34 percent felt the same way.

J. F. Sweeney [98]

There are a number of reasons why trust in the medical profession has declined in recent years, but one of them is likely the internet. While this tool can be a helpful source of information about health issues, it can also be a counterproductive one. Without a great deal of effort, for example, one can second guess any generally accepted medical advice. Vaccines? Forget it! According to some anti-vaxxer web sites, the medical profession is squelching information showing that vaccines cause autism in children.[99] Exercise and eat right to lose weight? Not necessary! Here is a site that guarantees huge weight loss just by taking a special supplement. Take prescription medicine to prevent recurring blood clots? The internet says we can reliably avoid them just by eating the right spices. And on, and on, and on.

Refusing a physician's advice just because we find something on the web that we would rather believe is self-sabotage. But this does not mean that the alternative is simply accepting what a doctor suggests. A more appropriate response is to understand the basis for a medical opinion, develop appropriate questions about its suitability for you, seek second opinions, and only then make an informed decision.

Doctors are sometimes wrong, but often a poorly-prepared patient should bear some of the blame. If we see doctors without preparing well, we will likely not get their best work. For example, without a prepared list of questions, an accurate description of our symptoms, and data (such as what we have been eating and when the symptoms occurred), we sabotage our chances of an accurate diagnosis.

We expect a doctor's best effort, and they, in turn, deserve our best effort as a patient.

Ignore the Dangers of High-Risk Activities

Not all high-risk activities involve extreme sports.

Most of us have experienced the high that comes with doing something that is a bit reckless. We all do it, especially when we are young. It is partly how we explore and understand the world and test ourselves. But experiencing something once is a lot different than making participation in high-risk activities a way of life.

When we think of high-risk activities, we are likely to focus on extreme sports such as base jumping and cave diving. But high risk can also be found without breaking a sweat. Using illicit drugs, promiscuity, driving recklessly, and binge drinking all qualify as well.

Perhaps we don't care about our own life, or believe that the high is worth the risk, or that precautions are for wimps. But we should all frequently remind ourselves that none of these activities ends with us. Our so-called joy rides can affect the lives of others as well as our own. Someone else has to clean up the mess that we create. That could mean, for example, providing lifetime care for our resulting disability, or coping with the financial and social consequences of drug use.

As noted earlier, one of the key capabilities that sets humans apart from most other animals is an ability to plan and project into the future and anticipate the consequences of actions. Tragedy can often be avoided by simply asking *what if?* and being honest and objective about the answer.

Live in Isolation

Even Tom Hanks needed someone to talk with.

People can be a pain in the neck, and sometimes it is best to get away from all of them for a while. Find a place in the woods. Turn off the cell phone. Kick back and enjoy the view.

While seclusion can be a perfectly good approach for a vacation, it is a lousy strategy for a good life. The more we isolate ourselves from others, the less feedback we get. And without that recalibration, we drift into a made-up world of our own prejudices and beliefs. In plain English, we get weird.

The movie *Castaway*, starred Tom Hanks as a modern-day Robinson Crusoe, but his co-star was arguably a volleyball named Wilson. Wilson was Hanks's sounding board, his effort to avoid becoming a true hermit.

There is good scientific evidence that having friends and social groups improves health. According to the Mayo Clinic:

- Friendships increase our sense of belonging and purpose.
- Friendships boost our happiness and reduce our stress.
- Friendships improve our self-confidence and self-worth.
- Friendships help us cope with traumas, such as divorce, serious illness, job loss, or the death of a loved one.
- Friendships encourage us to change or avoid unhealthy lifestyle habits, such as excessive drinking or lack of exercise.[100]

With low social interaction, we also tend to die younger. Brigham Young University researchers found, for example, that the effects of social isolation on mortality are comparable to those of alcoholism and smoking, and are worse than those of poor physical activity or obesity."[101]

Being social is not always easy. It will sometimes mean tolerating behaviors and opinions we may not like. We might find ourselves avoiding trivial confrontations by saying "you are probably right" more often than we really want to. But this is a small price to pay for a better life. As Yale Professor and author Paul Bloom writes: "Humans are social beings, and we are happier, and better, when connected to others."[102]

Get Trapped on the
Health Fringe

Black market rhinoceros horn goes for over $100,000 per kilogram because of unjustified beliefs that it is a cure for cancer and other problems.
G. Guilford [103]

People believe all sorts of unproven and dubious ideas, especially when it comes to their health. The healing power of rhinoceros horn is just one of a long line of fringe beliefs have their roots in ancient practices, pseudoscience, and conspiracy theories.

Clearly, those who believe in unproven treatments waste their hard-earned cash on things that don't deliver. But more importantly, those patients who really need medical help might opt for the myth rather than conventional treatment. A trip to an Asian apothecary for rhinoceros horn is not the same as seeking medical help at a good hospital.

Belief in fringe ideas such as crystal healing, homeopathy, the efficacy of rhinoceros horn, and the many other myths and questionable theories that surround health and disease can trap us in a mindset that feeds on itself and keeps us from seeking real help. We become victims of groupthink, often magnified by repeated and exclusive interactions with those having similar views.[104]

There is no reliable cure for this type of thinking. The key is how much we allow our health and nutrition to be dominated by poor thinking and baseless hope. When the consequences are important, we should always ask ourselves and others *what do we really know and how do we know it?*

Don't Plan for Our Own Demise

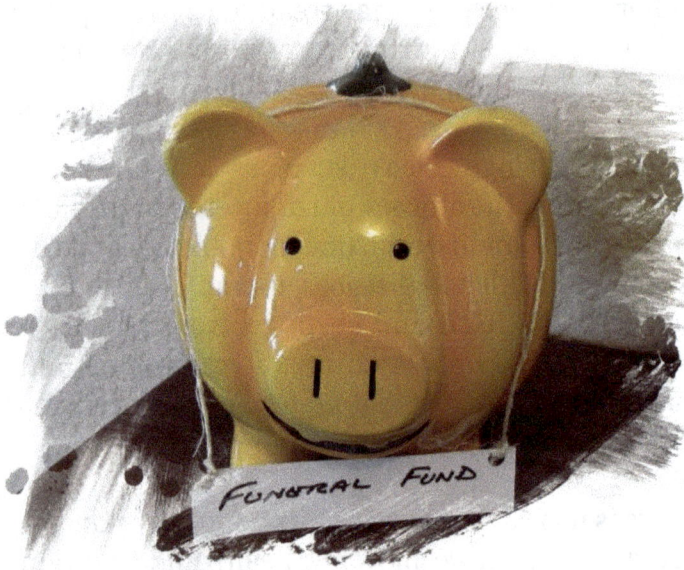

Life is pleasant. Death is peaceful. It's the transition that's troublesome.
Attributed to Isaac Asimov [105]

TV commercials for final expense life insurance may lead some to believe that dying is mostly about dealing with the cost of a funeral and paying off some outstanding debts. But that is highly misleading.

One issue that can go haywire, for example, is that our medical decisions might be made by someone we don't trust or who does not know us well.[106] Unless we have provided appropriate end-of-life instructions and medical power of attorney, the courts might decide who is in charge when we are incapacitated. Putting off such decisions not only causes us to lose control, but also puts heavy burdens on those who become responsible for us.

Making end-of-life health care decisions is difficult, and involves much more than handing a lawyer a credit card. Mostly, it requires a great deal of honest and deep thought. How do we want to be treated when we are dying? Should extraordinary measures be used to keep us alive, even if we will never be our old self again? Who should make medical decisions for us if we can't make them ourselves? Who do we want to handle our bills? Do we want a funeral?

Plans and preparation for death are best made when we are still mentally sharp. As we age, the ability to think clearly and not procrastinate becomes harder. Many of us never get to the details of dying, leaving relatives or friends with a mess. If we were kind to our friends and family in life, we should try to be kind to them in death.

Some Final Thoughts on Finding a Better Path

When we look back at some of the many ways that we can sabotage our lives, two basic themes emerge. One is that we don't live in bubbles with a nice cushion between us and the rest of the world. What we do impacts the lives of others. Not just family, friends, and coworkers, but anyone. Drive drunk and kill some poor stranger. Live casually and expect others to pick up the slack. Exploit others for our own convenience. Since we accomplish little on our own, treating others poorly is a really bad strategy.

The second theme is that many traits we possess have a balance point. Be selfish, but not too selfish. Work hard, but don't let work dominate our lives. Fight hard for rights, but don't forget the responsibilities that go with them. Many times, we sabotage ourselves not by doing or not doing something, but by doing too much or too little.

How do you think you stack up on these potential acts of self-sabotage? On a scale of 1 to 10, (1 being perfect and 10 meaning deep trouble), where do you think you lie, for example, on thinking negatively, becoming a couch potato, or failing to meet commitments?

One way to calibrate such an exercise might be to take a lesson from *New York Times* columnist David Brooks. He suggests imagining what might be said by others at our funeral or life celebration. He explains it this way:

It occurred to me that there were two sets of virtues, the resume virtues and the eulogy virtues. The resume virtues are the skills you bring to the marketplace. The eulogy virtues are the ones that are talked about at your funeral — whether you were kind, brave, honest or faithful. Were you capable of deep love?[107]

Our resumes strive to make the "what we did during our lives" more important than it really is. How we went about our lives, on the other hand, is a more enduring quality. What were our values? How responsible were we? Did our decisions and behaviors build or sabotage? These are the things that make a life worth celebrating and what those around the gravesite will remember.

About the Author

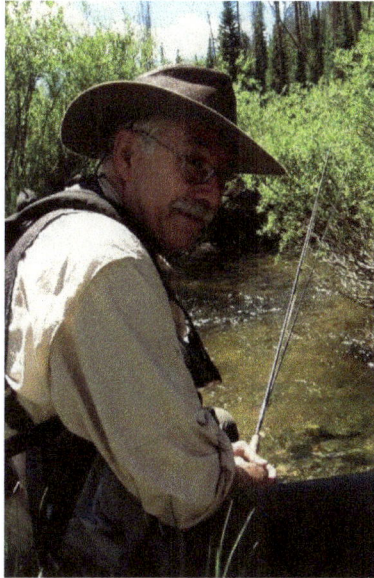

Greg Moore is a 25-year veteran of the Central Intelligence Agency where he spent his government career developing devices and concepts for use in Agency operations. He is a former Chief Scientist of the Agency's research office and a former Editor-in-Chief of *The Journal of Intelligence Community Research and Development.*

Prior to his government career, he held positions as an industrial research scientist with Masonite Corporation in Chicago, Illinois, and as an assistant professor at the Virginia Polytechnic Institute and State University in Blacksburg, Virginia.

He holds BS, MS, and PhD degrees from The Pennsylvania State University, University Park, Pennsylvania and a Master of Engineering Science degree from Loyola University, Baltimore, Maryland.

His prior books include: *Properties and Processing of Polymers for Engineers* (with D.E. Kline), *Failing Forward Fast: What 25 Years in the CIA Taught Us about Getting Things Done in Bureaucracies* (first and second editions with B. Hartmann), and *What Do We Know and How Do We Know It? Decision Making in a World of Vested Interests.* All are available on *Amazon.com*.

Photo Credits

Front Matter

The drawing used in this section is adapted from Ron Leishman/Shutterstock.com.

How We Think and Reason

The drawing in "Think Negatively" is adapted from Delcarmat/Shutterstock.com.

The drawing in "Believe That We Are Smarter Than Everyone Else" is adapted from Khakimullin Akeksandr/Shutterstock.com.

The drawing in "Pay No Attention to History" is adapted from a National Archives and Records Administration image of the first page of the U.S. Constitution.

The drawing in "Sacrifice the Future for the Now" is adapted from RIFE Stock/Shutterstock.com.

The drawing in "Choose Facts That Fit Our Biases" is adapted from GrAl/Shutterstock.com.

How We Treat Ourselves

The drawing in "Lie to Ourselves" is adapted from Darrin Henry/Shutterstock.com.

The drawing in "Waste Our Education" is adapted from Rido/Shutterstock.com.

The drawing in "Hang Out With the Wrong Crowd" is adapted from Motortion Films/Shutterstock.com.

The drawing in "Squander Our Time" is adapted from Pathdoc/Shutterstock.com.

The drawing in "Let Someone Else's Addiction Ruin Our Life" is adapted from Leszek Czerwonka/Shutterstock.com.

The drawing in "Defer Our Dreams Until 'Someday'" is adapted from Pikselstock/Shutterstock.com.

How We Treat Others

The drawing in "Fail to Control Our Emotions" is adapted from Moriz/Shutterstock.

The drawing in "Meddle in Other's Lives" is adapted from Evgenia Parajanian/Shutterstock.

The drawing in "Obsess Over Rights and Ignore Responsibilities" is adapted from Larry1235/Shutterstock.com.

The drawing in "Act Like a Know-It-All" is adapted from Ljupco Smokovski/Shutterstock.com.

The drawing in "Spend More Time Talking Than Listening" is adapted from Cate Frost/Shutterstock.com.

The drawing in "Fail to Launch" is adapted from Pressmaster/Shutterstock.com.

Work Lives

The drawing in "Never Graduate From High School" is adapted from Sherry Saye/Shutterstock.com.

The drawing in "Work for a Jerk" is adapted from Nattakorn_Maneerat/Shutterstock.com.

The drawing in "Steal From Employers" is adapted from Milan1983/Shutterstock.com.

The drawing in "Do Less Than Our Best" is adapted from Paul Vasarhelyi/Shutterstock.com.

The drawing in "Let Our Job Become Our Life" is adapted from Terd486/Shutterstock.com.

Finances

The drawing in "Maintain Balances on Credit Cards" is adapted from Stokkete/Shutterstock.com.

The drawing in "Put All of Our Eggs in One Basket" is adapted from art_of_sun/Shutterstock.com.

The drawing in "Play Roulette With Health Insurance" is adapted from Gorodenkoff/Shutterstock.com.

The drawing in "Have Children Too Early in Life" is adapted from Ink Drop/Shutterstock.com.

Health and Nutrition

The drawing in "Take Up Smoking" is adapted from Solid photos/Shutterstock.com.

The drawing in "Eat Whatever We Like" is adapted from Arabella Roberts/Shutterstock.com.

The drawing in "Handle Stress Poorly" is adapted from Vectorfusionart/Shutterstock.com.

The drawing in "Become a Couch Potato" is adapted from Alexander Raths/Shutterstock.com.

The drawing in "Disregard Our Doctor's Advice" is adapted from Didesign 021/Shutterstock.com.

End Notes

[1] Walt Kelly was an American cartoonist most famous for his comic strip, POGO. The strip featured a main character of the same name, and his fellow creatures who lived in the Okefenokee Swamp. The "we are us" comment is in reference to the earth's (then) 3.7 billion inhabitants and the environmental damage they were causing. The saying first appeared in an Earth Day poster done by Kelly in 1970 and later in the POGO comic strip in 1971.

[2] After a bad day, the bit of hope that "I will try again tomorrow" provides can make a big difference in how well we sleep that night and how we approach the problem the next day.

[3] Lao Tzu was a Chinese philosopher and the founder of Taoism. The quote is taken from *Goodreads website* accessed 3/2/2021, https://www.goodreads.com/quotes/8203490-watch-your-thoughts-they-become-your-words-watch-your-words

[4] Shermer, M., "The After Time, The Future of Civilization after COVID-19," *Skeptic Magazine*, Vol 26, No. 1, 2021.

[5] Isaac Asimov was an 20th century American author and scientist. Others (including some notable comedians) have said similar things. See, for example, *Quote Investigator website* accessed 3/2/2021, https://quoteinvestigator.com/2019/07/13/know-all/

[6] Kruger J., and Dunning, D., "Unskilled and Unaware of It: How Difficulties in Recognizing One's Own Incompetence Lead to Inflated Self-Assessments," *J Pers Soc Psychol,* December 1999; Vol. 77, No. 6, pp.1121-34.

Dunning, D., "The Dunning–Kruger Effect," *Advances in Experimental Social Psychology*, December 2011, Vol. 44, pp. 247-296.

[7] While this quote is frequently attributed to Franklin, there is some question whether he actually said it. For example, the first documented references to this quote by Franklin occurred well after his death.

[8] Emerson, R.W., *Essays on Courage*, Fields, Osgood & Co., Boston, 1870.

[9] Bayan, R., *The Cynic's Dictionary*, William Morrow, New York, 1994.

[10] Camera, L., "U.S. Students Show No Improvement in Math, Reading, Science on International Exam," *U. S. News website* accessed 3/2/2021,
https://www.usnews.com/news/education-news/articles/2019-12-03/us-students-show-no-improvement-in-math-reading-science-on-international-exam

[11] Because of the differences in time zones and start times, the Washington, DC train covers 140 miles (70 mph * 2 hrs) before the Chicago train starts. The problem then reduces to the simpler question of what time, t, the two meet on the remaining 624 miles. Both cover part of the ground in the remaining time, so the relationship is simply: 60mph * t + 70 mph * t = 624; or about 4.8 hours (the Chicago train travels 288 miles and the Baltimore train travels 336 miles in that time). Thus the point at which the two trains meet is east of Chicago about three-eighths of the total line distance (288/764). A map of of the Amtrak route puts the meeting place near Toledo.

[12] The reply was Franklin's response when asked in 1787 whether the Constitutional Convention had produced a republic or a monarchy.

[13] For an interesting perspective on the teaching of American history in high school, see Loewen, J., *Lies My Teacher Told Me*, The New Press, New York, 2018.

[14] The acronym SIFT was taken from the *Illinois Central College Library website* accessed 3/2/2021,
https://libguides.icc.edu/ld.php?content_id=14095894

[15] Daniel Kahneman is a Princeton University psychologist who won the Nobel Memorial Prize in Economic Sciences in 2002. *Thinking Fast and Slow* was published in 2011 by Farrar, Straus, and Giroux, New York, New York.

Dan Ariely is the James B. Duke Professor of Psychology and Behavioral Economics at Duke University. *Predictably Irrational: The Hidden Forces That Shape Our Decisions*, was published in 2009 by Harper Collins, New York, New York.

[16] Thomas Paul was a 19th century Baptist minister. The quote is taken from *Goodreads website* accessed 3/2/2021, https://www.goodreads.com/quotes/869818-life-is-a-series-of-mistakes-connected-by-failures-to

[17] Vo, L.T., "How Much Does The Government Spend To Send A Kid To Public School?" June 21, 2012, *National Public Radio website* accessed 3/2/2021, https://www.npr.org/sections/money/2012/06/21/155515613/how-much-does-the-government-spend-to-send-a-kid-to-school

[18] How well some teachers and public education systems encourage these critical skills is a topic best left for another day.

[19] From the 2002 movie, *Mr. Deeds*, starring Adam Sandler. For a description of the movie, see *Wikipedia website* accessed 3/2/2021, https://en.wikipedia.org/wiki/Mr._Deeds

[20] Park, W., "How Your Friends Change Your Habits - For Better and Worse," *BBC website* accessed 3/2/2021, https://www.bbc.com/future/article/20190520-how-your-friends-change-your-habits---for-better-and-worse

[21] James, W., *The Principles of Psychology, Vol.1,* Henry Holt and Company, New York, 1890.

[22] *Garbage in, garbage out*, is a phrase popularized by the computer industry. It is the idea that bad data produces bad results.

[23] Moran, A., "7 Ways to Overcome Toxic Self-Criticism," *Psychology Today website* accessed 3/2/2021, https://www.psychologytoday.com/us/blog/what-mentally-strong-people-dont-do/201801/7-ways-overcome-toxic-self-criticism

24 Schroeder, M. O., "Self-Criticism Can Be Psychologically Devastating – How to Overcome It," *US News and World Report*, March 17, 2016, *US News website* accessed 3/2/2021, https://health.usnews.com/wellness/articles/2016-03-17/self-criticism-can-be-psychologically-devastating-how-to-overcome-it

25 "Substance Abuse: Overview and Impact," Office of Disease Prevention and Health Promotion, *Healthypeople.gov website* accessed 3/2/2021, https://www.healthypeople.gov/2020/leading-health-indicators/2020-lhi-topics/Substance-Abuse

26 This gambling statistic is based on information from the *International Center for Responsible Gambling website,* citing that roughly 1% of adults (there are approximately 210,000,000 adults in the U.S.) have gambling disorders. This does not include children who have gambling problems. See, for example, "Gambling Disorders Fact Sheet," *International Center for Responsible Gaming website* accessed 3/2/2021, https://www.icrg.org/sites/default/files/oec/pdfs/ncrg_fact_sheet_gambling_disorders.pdf

27 Lipari, R.N., and S.L. Van Horn, "Children Living with Parents Who Have A Substance Use Disorder," *Substance Abuse and Mental Health Services Administration website* accessed 3/2/2021, https://www.samhsa.gov/data/sites/default/files/report_3223/ShortReport-3223.html

28 Sometimes, this decision can be the incentive needed for the addict to reform, but don't count on it. We are first and foremost responsible for ourselves and our children.

29 D'zurilla, C., "Taylor Swift: Never Give 'Em a Chance to Say You're 'Crazy'," February 4, 2014, *The Morning Call website* accessed 3/2/2021, https://www.mcall.com/la-et-mg-taylor-swift-glamour-magazine-20140204-story.html

30 From *All in the Family*, a television show that ran from 1971 to 1979 on CBS. The actual phrase was "stifle yourself." For a description of the show see *Wikipedia website* accessed 3/2/2021,

https://en.wikipedia.org/wiki/Archie_Bunker

[31] From a bumper sticker seen in Pueblo, Colorado. The quote is likely a parody of the J. R. R. Tolkien quote in *The Fellowship of the Ring*: "Do not meddle in the affairs of Wizards, for they are subtle and quick to anger."

[32] Hoffer, E., *The True Believer*, Harper and Brothers, New York, 1951.

[33] "Car Accident Statistics in the U.S.," *Driver Knowledge website* accessed 3/2/2021, https://www.driverknowledge.com/car-accident-statistics/

Approximately 94% of all automobile accidents are caused by human error. See, for example, Singh, S., "Critical reasons for crashes investigated in the National Motor Vehicle Crash Causation Survey," (Traffic Safety Facts Crash•Stats. Report No. DOT HS 812 115), *National Highway Traffic Safety Administration website* accessed 3/2/2021, https://crashstats.nhtsa.dot.gov/Api/Public/ViewPublication/812115

[34] Forum on Child and Family Statistics, "Number of Children (in millions) Ages 0-17 in the United States by Age, 1950–2019 and Projected 2020–2050," *Childstats.gov website* accessed 5/6/2021, https://www.childstats.gov/americaschildren/tables/pop1.asp

[35] National Center for Health Statistics, "Births and Natality," *Centers for Disease Control and Prevention website* accessed 5/6/2021, https://www.cdc.gov/nchs/fastats/births.htm

[36] "Facts About Child Hunger in America," *NoKidHungry website* accessed 3/31/2021, https://www.nokidhungry.org/who-we-are/hunger-facts

[37] "National Statistics On Child Abuse," *National Children's Alliance website* accessed 3/31/2021, https://www.nationalchildrensalliance.org/media-room/national-statistics-on-child-abuse/

[38] "44 Percent of Custodial Parents Receive the Full Amount of Child Support." *United States Census Bureau website* accessed 3/31/2021, https://www.census.gov/newsroom/press-releases/2018/cb18-tps03.html

[39] "Parents 2017:Unleashing Their Power & Potential," Survey Report, *Learning Heroes website* accessed 3/31/2021, https://bealearninghero.org/research/

[40] Curley, B., "Prediabetes Is on the Rise in Children — What Can We Do to Stop It?" December 9, 2019, *Healthline website* accessed 3/31/2021, https://www.healthline.com/health-news/diabetes-children-rising-how-stop-it

[41] Churchill, W., a speech given September 6, 1943 at Harvard University. *International Churchill Society website* accessed 3/2/2021, https://winstonchurchill.org/resources/speeches/1941-1945-war-leader/the-price-of-greatness-is-responsibility/

[42] Jami, C., *Killosophy: Killing Knowledge, Loving Wisdom*, Criss Jami, 2015.

[43] Boghossian, P., and J. Lindsay, *How to Have Impossible Conversations*, Hatchette, New York, 2019.

[44] Carnegie, D., *How to Win Friends and Influence People*, Simon & Schuster, New York, 1936.

[45] Although this quote is often attributed to Mark Twain, and occasionally to Abraham Lincoln, it most likely originated in Maurice Switzer's book, *Mrs. Goose, Her Book* (Moffat, Yard & Company, New York, 1907). *Quote Investigator website* accessed 3/2/2021, https://quoteinvestigator.com/2010/05/17/remain-silent/

[46] "Bernard M. Baruch Quotes," *Goodreads website* accessed 3/2/2021, https://www.goodreads.com/author/quotes/5768330.Bernard_M_Baruch

47 Paine, A.B., *Mark Twain: A Biography,* Project Gutenberg ebook #2988, August 21, 2006, *The Project Gutenberg website* accessed 3/2/2021, https://www.gutenberg.org/files/2988/2988-h/2988-h.htm

48 Stephens, R., J. Atkins, and A. Kinsgton, "Swearing as a Response to Pain," *NeuroReport,* August 2009, Vol. 20, No. 12, pp. 1056-1060.

49 Lewis, J.P., "Forbidden Words," *Torch Magazine,* Fall 2016, *North Carolina Sociological Association website* accessed 3/2/2021, http://www.ncsociology.org/torchmagazine/v901/Lewis.pdf

50 Mike Royer is an American comic artist. The quote is taken from *Quotetab website* accessed 5/6/2021, https://www.quotetab.com/quotes/by-mike-royer

51 "Speak When You're Angry and You'll Make the Best Speech You'll Ever Regret," *Quote Investigator website* accessed 3/2/2021, https://quoteinvestigator.com/tag/ambrose-bierce/

52 Mayo Clinic Staff, "Anger Management: 10 Tips to Tame Your Temper," *Mayo Clinic website* accessed 3/2/2021, https://www.mayoclinic.org/healthy-lifestyle/adult-health/in-depth/anger-management/art-20045434

53 See, for example, At the Crossroads, *At The Crossroads web site* accessed 3/2/2021, https://www.atthecrossroads.com/g/Failure-To-Launch-Programs-For-Young-Adults/Colorado-CO/

54 U.S. Bureau of Labor Statistics, "The Economics Daily, Median Weekly Earnings $606 for High School Dropouts, $1,559 for Advanced Degree Holders," October 21, 2019, *U.S. Bureau of Labor Statistics website* accessed 3/2/2021, https://www.bls.gov/opub/ted/2019/median-weekly-earnings-606-for-high-school-dropouts-1559-for-advanced-degree-holders.htm

55 Fight Crime: Invest in Kids, "School or the Streets, Crime and America's Dropout Crisis," *Alabama Partnership for Children website* accessed 3/2/2021,

https://alabamapartnershipforchildren.org/wp-content/uploads/2016/12/School-or-the-Streets-Crime-and-Americas-Dropout-Crisis.pdf

56 Doll, J. D., Z. Eslami, and L. Walters, "Understanding Why Students Drop Out of High School, According to Their Own Reports: Are They Pushed or Pulled, or Do They Fall Out?" *Sage journals website* accessed 3/2/2021, https://Journals.sagepub.com

57 Outside organizations that offer help include the Boys & Girls Clubs of America and Big Brothers Big Sisters of America.

58 Robert Sutton is the author of *The No-Asshole Rule*, Hatchette, New York, 2007. The statement comes from an interview with Sutton that was published in Illing, S., "A Stanford Psychologist on the Art of Avoiding Assholes," *Vox website* accessed 3/2/2021, https://www.vox.com/conversations/2017/9/26/16345476/stanford-psychologist-art-of-avoiding-assholes

59 Elliott, C., "Warren Buffett Quotes: 37 Lessons from the Oracle of Omaha," *Listen Money Matters website* accessed 4/23/2021, https://www.listenmoneymatters.com/warren-buffett-quotes/

Although Warren Buffett meant this in the context of deciding whether to hold or sell underperforming stocks, it seems a good analogy to decisions about continuing or abandoning a career that is not meeting our goals and needs.

60 Magic Johnson is a former professional basketball player. This quote is taken from the *Goodreads website* accessed 3/2/2021, https://www.goodreads.com/quotes/7380156-talent-is-never-enough-with-few-exceptions-the-best-players

61 Both-Nwabuwe, J. M. C., M. T. M. Dijkstra, and B. Beersma, "Sweeping the Floor or Putting a Man on the Moon: How to Define and Measure Meaningful Work," 2017, *Frontiers in Psychology website* accessed 6/6/2021, https://www.frontiersin.org/articles/10.3389/fpsyg.2017.01658/full

[62] Howes, L., "20 Lessons from Walt Disney on Entrepreneurship, Innovation and Chasing Your Dreams," *Forbes website* accessed 3/2/2021, https://www.forbes.com/sites/lewishowes/2012/07/17/20-business-quotes-and-lessons-from-walt-disney/?sh=218b1bf24ba9

[63] Achor, S. and M. Gielan, "The Data-Driven Case for Vacation," *Harvard Business Review*, July 13, 2016 *HBR website* accessed 4/3/2021, https://hbr.org/2016/07/the-data-driven-case-for-vacation

[64] Sampson, H., "What Does America Have Against Vacation?" August 28, 2019. *Washington Post website* accessed 3/2/2021, https://www.washingtonpost.com/travel/2019/08/28/what-does-america-have-against-vacation/

[65] Adapted from Covey, S., *Seven Habits of Highly Successful People*, Free Press, New York, 2004.

[66] These estimates were taken from an online crowd-sourced database in which users in different locations around the world share information about cost of living and other quality of life factors. The estimates were not independently verified. *Numbeo website* accessed 3/2/2021, https://www.numbeo.com/cost-of-living/in/Denver

[67] Huddleston, C., "Survey: 69% of Americans Have Less Than $1,000 in Savings," December 16, 2019, *GoBankingRates website* accessed 3/2/2021, https://www.gobankingrates.com/saving-money/savings-advice/americans-have-less-than-1000-in-savings/

[68] A good exercise is to think through the other Starbucks-like expenses in our lives that drain income. Some examples are: cell phone plans, gym memberships, recurring app costs, eating out, etc.

[69] For simplicity, the calculation ignores potential complications such as the effect of unemployment on retirement contributions and health insurance costs.

[70] "The Eighth Wonder of the World Is Compound Interest," *Quote Investigator website* accessed 6/6/2021, https://quoteinvestigator.com/2019/09/09/interest/#:~:text=Apocryphal%3F,eighth%20wonder%20of%20the%20world.

[71] Irby, L., "The Cost of Paying Off Debt with Minimum Payments," *The Balance website* accessed 6/5/2021, https://www.thebalance.com/how-long-to-pay-off-balance-with-minimum-payments-961120

[72] Based on the results of the credit card minimum balance calculator provided by Bankrate, *Bankrate.com website* accessed 6/6/2021, https://www.bankrate.com/calculators/credit-cards/credit-card-minimum-payment.aspx

For an explanation of how credit card interest works, see Steele, J., "How Does Credit Card Interest Work?" September 4, 2019, *Experion website* accessed 4/3/2021, https://www.experian.com/blogs/ask-experian/how-does-credit-card-interest-work/

[73] Keisler-Starkey, K., and L. N. Bunch, "Health Insurance Coverage in the United States: 2019,"Current Population Reports, September 2020. *United States Census Bureau website* accessed 3/2/2021, https://www.census.gov/content/dam/Census/library/publications/2020/demo/p60-271.pdf

[74] Himmelstein, D.U., R. M. Lawless, D. Thorne, P. Foohey, and S. Woolhandler, "Medical Bankruptcy: Still Common Despite the Affordable Care Act," *American Journal of Public Health*, March 2019. *American Journal of Public Health website* accessed 3/2/2021, https://ajph.aphapublications.org/doi/abs/10.2105/AJPH.2018.304901?journalCode=ajph&

[75] "How Much Does A Broken Arm Cost?" *Cost Helper Health website* accessed 4/3/2021, https://health.costhelper.com/broken-arm.html

[76] "Report on the Economic Well-Being of U.S. Households in 2018 - May 2019," *Federal Reserve website* accessed 4/2021,

https://www.federalreserve.gov/publications/2019-economic-well-being-of-us-households-in-2018-dealing-with-unexpected-expenses.htm

[77] Lankford, K., "Health Insurance Options After You Lose Your Job," April 6, 2020, American Association of Retired Persons, *AARP website* accessed 4/3/2021, https://www.aarp.org/health/health-insurance/info-2020/job-loss-options.html

[78] Powell, F., and E. Kerr, "See the Average College Tuition in 2020-2021," *U.S. News website* accessed 3/2/2021, https://www.usnews.com/education/best-colleges/paying-for-college/articles/paying-for-college-infographic

[79] Helhoski, A., and R. Lane, "2020 Student Loan Debt Statistics," *Nerdwallet website* accessed 3/2/2021, https://www.nerdwallet.com/blog/loans/student-loans/student-loan-debt/

[80] Samuel, S., "How College Loans Exploit Students for Profits," *TED website* accessed 3/2/2021, https://www.ted.com/talks/sajay_samuel_how_college_loans_exploit_students_for_profit?language=en#t-50688

[81] "The 20 Best - and Worst - Paid College Majors," *Time website* accessed 3/2/2021, http://content.time.com/time/specials/packages/completelist/0,29569,2073703,00.html

[82] Bidwell, A., "Student Loan Expectations: Myth vs. Reality," *U.S. News website* accessed 3/2/2021, https://www.usnews.com/news/blogs/data-mine/2014/10/07/student-loan-expectations-myth-vs-reality

[83] Anonymous, "James Taylor Covers Timeless Songs in 'American Standard'," *American Association of Retired Persons website* accessed 3/2/2021, https://www.aarp.org/entertainment/music/info-2020/james-taylor-american-standard.html

[84] Kershaw, S., "Now, the Bad News on Teenage Marriage," *New York Times website* accessed 3/2/2021, https://www.nytimes.com/2008/09/04/fashion/04marriage.html

[85] Katy Suellentrop, K., "The Costs and Consequences of Teen Childbearing," August 17, 2010, The National Campaign to Prevent Teen and Unplanned Pregnancy, *Center for Disease Control website* accessed 3/2/2021, https://www.cdc.gov/nchs/ppt/nchs2010/29_suellentrop.pdf

[86] U.S. Department of Agriculture, "The Cost of Raising a Child," *U. S. Department of Agriculture website* accessed 3/2/20221, https://www.usda.gov/media/blog/2017/01/13/cost-raising-child

[87] "Plans are Worthless, but Planning is Everything," *Quote Investigator website* accessed 3/2/2021, https://quoteinvestigator.com/2017/11/18/planning/Eisenhower

[88]Center for Disease Control and Prevention, "Smoking and Tobacco Use Quick Facts," *Center for Disease Control and Prevention website* accessed 3/2/2021, https://www.cdc.gov/tobacco/data_statistics/fact_sheets/fast_facts/index.htm

[89]Smokefree.gov, "How Much Will You Save?" *Smokefree website* accessed 3/2/2021, https://smokefree.gov/quit-smoking/why-you-should-quit/how-much-will-you-save

[90] Michael was a 1996 film about several distressed people and the archangel who came to help them. See, for example, its entry in the *Wikipedia website* accessed 3/2/2021, https://en.wikipedia.org/wiki/Michael_(1996_film)

[91], Office of Disease Prevention and Health Promotion, "Dietary Guidelines 2015-2020," *Health.gov website* accessed 3/2/2021, https://health.gov/our-work/food-nutrition/2015-2020-dietary-guidelines/guidelines/message/

[92] Price, C., "The Age of Scurvy," August 14, 2017, *Science History Institute website* accessed 6/62021, https://www.sciencehistory.org/distillations/the-age-of-scurvy

[93] Mayo Clinic, "Vitamins and Minerals: What You Should Know About Essential Nutrients," *Mayo Clinic website* accessed 7/10/2021, https://www.mayoclinic.org/documents/mc5129-0709-sp-rpt-pdf/doc-20079085

[94] Mayo Clinic, "Nutrition and Healthy Eating," *Mayo Clinic website* accessed 3/2/2021, https://www.mayoclinic.org/healthy-lifestyle/nutrition-and-healthy-eating/basics/nutrition-basics/hlv-20049477

National Agricultural Library, Food and Nutrition Information Center, *USDA website* accessed 6/6/2021, https://www.nal.usda.gov/fnic

[95] Nutrition is a business that often sells more hope than scientifically-sound advice. If a source provides advice that is far from what is generally accepted, remember that it is up to them to prove their case, not for others to disprove it. As the astronomer, Carl Sagan, often noted: extraordinary claims require extraordinary proof. A handful of carefully selected anecdotes or testimonials does not constitute proof.

[96] Mayo Clinic, "Need stress relief? Try the 4 A's," *Mayo Clinic website* accessed 6/6/2021, https://www.mayoclinic.org/healthy-lifestyle/stress-management/in-depth/stress-relief/art-20044476

[97] The Center for Disease Control and Prevention keeps track of lifestyle trends through their Behavioral Risk Factor Surveillance System. In telephone surveys, they ask the following question: "During the past month, other than your regular job, did you participate in any physical activities or exercises such as running, calisthenics, golf, gardening, or walking for exercise?" In many of the southern states (including Kentucky, Tennessee, Alabama, Mississippi, and Louisiana), 30% or more of adults answered "no.". Colorado, Utah, Washington, and Oregon, on the other hand, were the most physically active states, with respondents reporting 17-20% inactivity. See, for example, Adult Physical Inactivity Prevalence Maps by Race/Ethnicity, *Center for Disease Control website* accessed 3/2/2021, https://www.cdc.gov/physicalactivity/data/inactivity-prevalence-maps/index.html

155

[98] Sweeney, J.F., "The Eroding Trust between Patients and Physicians," April 10, 2018 , *Medial Economics website* accessed 3/2/2021, https://www.medicaleconomics.com/medical-economics-blog/eroding-trust-between-patients-and-physicians

[99] The controversy over vaccines gained strength when a British doctor and his colleagues published results of a small study linking the measles, mumps, and rubella (MMR) vaccine to autism in young children. The work was fraudulent, and subsequently retracted by *The Lancet.* (see "RETRACTED: Ileal-lymphoid-nodular hyperplasia, non-specific colitis, and pervasive developmental disorder in children, " *The Lancet website* accessed 3/2/2010, https://www.thelancet.com/journals/lancet/article/PIIS0140-6736(97)11096-0/fulltext

[100] Mayo Clinic Staff, "Friendships: Enrich Your Life and Improve Your Health," *Mayo Clinic website* accessed 3/2/2021, https://www.mayoclinic.org/healthy-lifestyle/adult-health/in-depth/friendships/art-20044860

[101] Holt-Lunstad, J., T. B. Smith, and J. B. Layton, "Social Relationships and Mortality Risk: A Meta-analytic Review," *PLoS Medicine*, July 27, 2010, Vol. 7, No. 7, *PLOS Medicine website* accessed 6/6/2021, https://journals.plos.org/plosmedicine/article?id=10.1371/journal.pmed.1000316

[102] Bloom, P., "Does Religion Make You Nice? Does Atheism Make You Mean?" *University of British Columbia website* accessed 3/2/2021, https://www2.psych.ubc.ca/~ara/media/Slate_article.pdf

[103] Guilford, G., "Why Does a Rhino Horn Cost $300,000? Because Vietnam Thinks It Cures Cancer and Hangovers," May 15, 2013, *The Atlantic website* accessed 3/2/2021, https://www.theatlantic.com/business/archive/2013/05/why-does-a-rhino-horn-cost-300-000-because-vietnam-thinks-it-cures-cancer-and-hangovers/275881/

[104] Some seemingly weird things do turn out to be true, At one time, for example, ideas such as rocks falling from the sky and continents moving were considered crazy. Then humans

156

discovered meteorites and tectonic plates. But such examples do not mean that all weird things will eventually be proven to be true once we are sufficiently enlightened.

[105] Asimov was an American science fiction writer. Some of his works include *I Robot* and *The Foundation Series.*

[106] While this discussion is focused on health issues, there are other considerations. When we die without a will, for example, the courts appoint someone to administer our estate, and distribute our assets according to a set formula. Whatever preferences we might have had no longer count. A distant relative could wind up with our assets rather than our unmarried partner, our friends, or our favorite charities.

[107] Brooks, D., "The Moral Bucket List," April 11, 2015, *The New York Times website* accessed 3/2/2021, https://www.nytimes.com/2015/04/12/opinion/sunday/david-brooks-the-moral-bucket-list.html

www.ingramcontent.com/pod-product-compliance
Lightning Source LLC
Chambersburg PA
CBHW071224290326
41931CB00037B/1955